SPINNING SPIDER

HAIKU OF RON PAPANDREA

1st Edition

SPINNING SPIDER

HAIKU OF RON PAPANDREA

1St Edition
Printed on acid-free paper
Published by Lightning Source
An Ingram Company
La Vergne, Tennessee, USA
Kiln Farm, Milton Keynes, UK

LCCN: 2013905113

ISBN: 978-0-9746527-9-5

Retail Price: $18.59 USD, £13.39 GBP, €14.99 EUR

Available from all major English language book
distributors with 55% wholesale discount
and returns accepted.

For Nancy

The Creation Poem

God hath hurled his stones in space
The ones that are real we can measure their pace
But those that move in merely the mind
There can be no measurement of any kind
And though I believe no God may be
And we're not made for eternity
I still tend to the stones of the great mystery

moving with the air

the first silk thread of a web

spinning its spider

I can see the lights

of cities at night; but drive

for the moon and stars

joy, rapture, music

the shadow of the dancer

flickers on the floor

peaks of snow and ice

a floating mountain lightly

on a sea of fog

spanning the waters

between nothing and nowhere

a bridge weakening

stepping on snowflakes

snowflakes covering my steps

winter in my heart

the gold light of day

is only there to make way

for the silver night

walking in the night

over the hill village lights

small stars on the ground

with each religion

the one true god

with no religion

soaring and sinking

with little children running

a kite flies the earth

there is a dance room

in a Tangier hotel; now

the drum is beating

red, orange, yellow, blue

rainbow arch across the road

sun in my mirror

people are dying

and yet you want to create

one more consiousness

haiku for each month

haiku readers look at me

twelve chickens no eggs

lines of lightning flash

linking the earth to the sky

the spirit camp speaks

times sphere grows larger

its inner sphere shrinks smaller

time creates space

looking at the sky

a butterfly of the night

alights on my ledge

it's a sacrifice

walking up the mountain path

to the high places

night sky bright as day

but silver beams are drawn thin

the stars move away

in the zen garden

the stone behind the mountain

I cannot see it

in the quiet night

my heart searches for your heart

and is satisfied

in the walled city

wandering, I found a place

where I lost my self

people are sinful

and in need of redemption

please drop dead prophets

fragments on the floor

too broken to be restored

a lost masterpiece

barks, yelps and laughter

chasing through the woods at night

running with the dogs

black night black highway

the road rounds a dark mountain

lights of a city

by cherry blossoms

I see your arm, you see mine

will we meet again?

a stone skips across

our moment of awareness

equally precious

a small butterfly

flying, fluttering, floating

in eye of the storm

world weary hours

a tired out traveler

finds his final breath

a perfect haiku

that explained the mystery

but not written down

across the divide

and to the rim of the world

I look over the edge

bright lights in the bus

moving through morning darkness

awake while asleep

a Guatemalan

has told us there is a God

he is very small

space bends, twists and curves

and we can't go everywhere

thoughts go anywhere

spin Timmy the Top

by the jukebox with arms cocked

spin Timmy the Top

scent of lavender

by candle light a monk's girl

the two enlightened

the earth the mountains

the water the sky; cradle

a perfect child

there may be a light

at the end of the tunnel

but the light is black

the orange sun rises

and the orange sun sets; submit

to the mystery

little hairy flea

jumping and happy to be

choked by the powder

grandfather bend down

to hear me. I am a small

voice. Take me with you

at this bar "Teasers"

it is said: "The worse it gets,

the better it gets"

breasts juggle – colors

laugh and cry – words sweet and sad

Stettner is stroking

www.ingramcontent.com/pod-product-compliance
Lightning Source LLC
Chambersburg PA
CBHW060743100426
42813CB00027B/3032